ROSS LYNCH

By Marie Morreale

Children's Press®
An Imprint of Scholastic Inc.

Photos ©: Patrick R. Murphy/Getty Images; back cover: Brendon Thorne/Getty Images; 1: Joey Terrill Photography; 2-3: John Lamparski/Getty Images; 4-5: Joey Terrill Photography; 6-7 background: Patrick R. Murphy/Getty Images; 7 left: Bryan Smith/Zuma Press; 7 right: Joey Terrill Photography; 8: Astrid Stawiarz/Getty Images; 10: John Lamparski/Getty Images; 11: Boston Globe/Getty Images; 12: Helga Esteb/Shutterstock, Inc.; 13 top: Suljo/Dreamstime; 13 center left: Michael Leonhard/age fotostock/Superstock, Inc.; 13 bottom: Lbarn/Dreamstime; 13 center right: Cosmin Sava/Shutterstock, Inc.; 14: Joey Terrill Photography; 15 top left: matt_scherf/iStockphoto; 15 top right: AF archive/Alamy Images; 15 bottom left: Phil Dent/Getty Images; 15 bottom right: Isselee/Dreamstime; 16: Ben Horton/Getty Images; 18 top: Pictorial Press Ltd/Alamy Images; 18 bottom: PacificCoastNews/Newscom; 19 top: infusny-146/INFphoto.com/Newscom; 19 bottom: Joey Terrill Photography; 20: Shirlaine Forrest/Getty Images; 21 top: Kevin Winter/Getty Images; 21 bottom: Alberto E. Rodriguez/Getty Images; 22 top: Barry Brecheisen/Getty Images; 22 bottom: Matt Sayles/Invision/AP Images; 23 top: Michael N. Todaro/Getty Images; 23 bottom: Everett Collection/Rex USA; 24: Michael N. Todaro/Getty Images; 25: Fox/Getty Images; 26, 28: Joey Terrill Photography; 29: Brendon Thorne/Getty Images; 30: Joey Terrill Photography; 31: Harry Woods/Getty Images; 32, 33, 35: Joey Terrill Photography; 36 background and throughout: conejota/Thinkstock; 36 main: Paul A. Hebert/Invision/AP Images; 37 paper background: Nonnakrit/Shutterstock, Inc.; 37 pushpin and throughout: seregam/Thinkstock; 37 French toast: Lana Langlois/Dreamstime; 37 oatmeal: Elena Elisseeva/Dreamstime; 37 sign: Ken Wolter/Shutterstock, Inc.; 37 sandwich: Ppy2010ha/Dreamstime; 37 Skittles: Roman Samokhin/Shutterstock, Inc.; 37 gummy bears: Ajafoto/Dreamstime; 38-39 spread: Joey Terrill Photography; 38 top left: PRPP_PRPP/Newscom; 38 top right, 38 bottom left, 38 bottom right, 39 top: Sultana/Splash News/Newscom; 40 background: My Life Graphic/Shutterstock, Inc.; 40 main: David Livingston/Getty Images; 41 top background: Nonnakrit/Shutterstock, Inc.; 41 bottom background: My Life Graphic/Shutterstock, Inc.; 41 inset: Paul Archuleta/Getty Images; 42: Patrick R. Murphy/Getty Images; 43: Helen Boast/Getty Images; 44: John Stillwell/EMPPL PA Wire/AP Images; 45: Joey Terrill Photography.

Library of Congress Cataloging-in-Publication Data
Morreale, Marie, author.
 Ross Lynch / by Marie Morreale.
  pages cm. — (Real bios)
 Includes bibliographical references and index.
 ISBN 978-0-531-21573-9 (library binding : alk. paper) —
ISBN 978-0-531-21665-1 (pbk. : alk. paper)
 1. Lynch, Ross, 1995– —Juvenile literature. 2. Rock musi-
cians—United States—Juvenile literature. I. Title.
 ML3930.L89 2015
 782.42164092—dc23 [B]   2014049196

© 2016 Scholastic Inc.

Printed in the United States 113
SCHOLASTIC, CHILDREN'S PRESS, and associated logos are trademarks and/or registered trademarks of Scholastic Inc.

1 2 3 4 5 6 7 8 9 10 R 25 24 23 22 21 20 19 18 17 16

MEET ROSS!

SINGER . . . R5 BAND MEMBER . . . ACTOR . . . AND MUCH MORE!

Nineteen-year-old Colorado native Ross Lynch has known exactly what he wanted to do with his life ever since he was a toddler. Even then, Ross was singing, dancing, and making people smile. He's achieved a lot in a few short years. He's a member of the hot band R5 and the star of the Disney Channel sitcom *Austin & Ally* and the *Teen Beach Movie* series. But even though he is a superstar, he is also a regular guy. This *Real Bio* will give you a glimpse of the real Ross. It's packed with quotes, trivia, and photos that will make you laugh. Did you know that Ross dreams of directing movies? That certain movies scare him? That he wants to become a pilot? Turn the pages of this book to read all about this explosive entertainer!

Ross sings from his heart! He wants to please his fans.

CONTENTS

Chill time! Ross takes a moment to relax between interviews.

ROCKING ROSS

FROM COLORADO TO CALIFORNIA IN SEARCH OF STARDOM!

Ross Shor Lynch was a late Christmas present for his parents, Stormie and Mark Lynch. He was born on December 29, 1995, and welcomed with love and laughter to the already thriving Lynch family. He had two older brothers named Riker and Rocky and an older sister named Rydel. Later on, Ross's younger brother Ryland rounded out the family.

The Lynches lived in Littleton, Colorado, where Mark was a successful businessman. He owned a company that supplied high-tech equipment for beauty salons and spas. Stormie was a stay-at-home mom who happily took care of the little Lynches. From the very beginning, the couple knew that their blond babies were very special. Stormie and Mark had always wanted to have a large family of unique children.

Whether it's just Ross or Ross and R5, there's fun to be had!

R5 checks out NYC from the Empire State Building's observation deck.

(L to R) R5—Rocky Lynch, Ross Lynch, Ellington Ratliff, Rydel Lynch, and Riker Lynch.

"I knew when I was having kids that I wanted them to have matching letters," Stormie told *Bop* magazine. "I thought Riker was going to be a girl, so I was going to use the letter 'M' and start with Madison. But the night before he was born, I thought, 'I feel like it's a boy!' And Mark, their dad, loved the movie *Star Trek*. So we named him after the character Commander Riker. Then, Rydel was named after Rydel High, the school from the movie *Grease*, which Mark and I watched all the time! When I was having Rocky, I told Riker, 'I'm having a new baby brother for you.' He was like, 'Call him Rocky!' after his fave baseball team, the Colorado Rockies. The whole family started calling him that so I had to name him Rocky. . . . And I always loved the name Ross.

"I used to work at a nail salon and an adorable little boy would come in named Ross, and I just thought it was the cutest name." Stormie didn't reveal the origins of youngest brother Ryland's name, but she did explain that her nickname for him is Best Boy.

At any rate, by the time Ryland was born, everyone knew his older siblings were natural-born entertainers. They all sang, danced, and played musical instruments. Ross recalled that he was especially fascinated by dance when he was younger. "I've been dancing for just about ever," he told *Bop*. "I've gone to dance studios and studied ballet, tap—pretty much every dance style!"

Stormie noticed Ross's special energy early on. "He would always be tapping his feet and dancing, even at the dinner table!" she told *Bop* magazine. So as she did with the other kids, she encouraged Ross to follow his dreams.

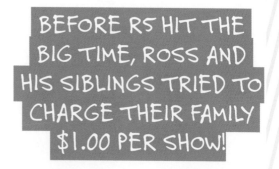

BEFORE R5 HIT THE BIG TIME, ROSS AND HIS SIBLINGS TRIED TO CHARGE THEIR FAMILY $1.00 PER SHOW!

Ross knew that he wanted to be a musical artist. He sang, he danced, and he taught himself to play the guitar. The four oldest Lynch kids formed a group and performed for their family and friends. They soon realized that music could be more than a hobby. This became especially clear one day when a middle-school-aged Ross was in a restaurant with his family. He told *J-14* magazine, "I was singing a song in a restaurant and this couple came up to me and said, 'You're going to be big one day,' and they asked me for my autograph!"

Little did that couple know how right they were! Their encouraging comment helped to steer Ross and his siblings toward the spotlight. "When I was younger, my brothers and I used to perform full-out dance numbers in our basement, usually to Michael Jackson songs," Ross told *Twist* magazine. "We watched almost every live video and learned every dance and the lyrics to every song! We performed for our friends and family and even tried to charge them to watch us, but it didn't work out that well, LOL! So we were like, 'No, we just want to perform. It doesn't matter,' and kept putting on shows almost every day for our family."

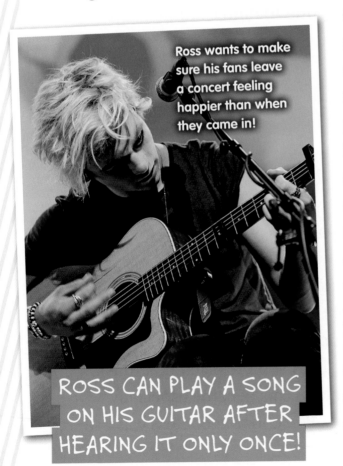

Ross wants to make sure his fans leave a concert feeling happier than when they came in!

ROSS CAN PLAY A SONG ON HIS GUITAR AFTER HEARING IT ONLY ONCE!

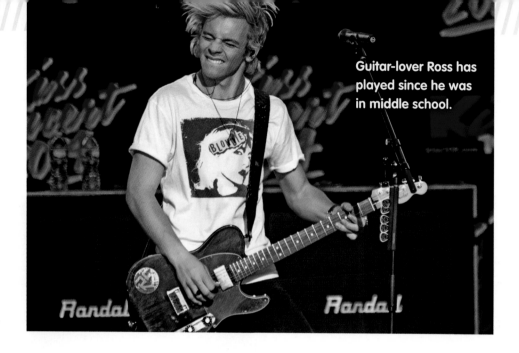

Guitar-lover Ross has played since he was in middle school.

When Ross was in fourth grade, he and his siblings started being homeschooled. This left them with plenty of time to practice their shows. They soon began expanding their audiences. "We actually joined a choir, like a glee club," Ross told *Twist* magazine. "We would go to old folks' homes, or perform at the mall—anywhere that would let us!"

It soon became obvious to Stormie and Mark that their kids were really talented, so they decided to relocate the family to Los Angeles, California, the center of the entertainment industry. This move was major. It gave the kids an opportunity to **audition** for TV shows, films, and music videos. Ross quickly started making his mark. In 2009, he appeared on *So You Think You Can Dance*. He also showed up in the Kidz Bop video for "Let It Rock" and Cymphonique's video for "Lil' Miss Swagger." That same year, the Lynch family met Ellington Ratliff at a dance studio. A born-and-bred California boy, Ellington fit right in with Riker, Rydel, Rocky, and Ross. The Lynches soon realized that their new friend would be a perfect addition to their music group. That's when they officially became R5 (good thing Ellington's last name began with an R!).

Before long, the Lynches were taking over in Hollywood. Riker starred as Jeff on *Glee* in 2010. The next year, Ross won the role of Austin Moon on

THE BASICS

Song Man
Ross sang all 14 songs on the Austin & Ally soundtrack album.

INSTRUMENTS: Guitar, bass, drums, and piano

DREAM ACTIVITY: To fly a plane

FULL NAME: Ross Shor Lynch

BIRTHDAY: December 29, 1995

BIRTHPLACE: Littleton, Colorado

COLLECTION: Guitars— his favorite guitar is named Luna

MUSICAL INFLUENCES: Elvis Presley, George Harrison of the Beatles

TOP 100: Named to Us magazine's 2012 Top 100 Cutest Guys

CHILDHOOD FEAR: Roller coasters

DREAM SUPERPOWER: To be able to fly

PERSONAL QUOTE: "Music is poetry with personality."

FAMILY VACAY DESTINATION: Skiing in Keystone, Colorado

DREAM CAR: A vintage muscle car

PASTIMES: Flying model airplanes, drawing and sketching, playing video games

the Disney Channel's *Austin & Ally*. In 2013, he also performed as Brady in the Disney Channel Original Movie *Teen Beach Movie*.

In between their acting gigs, the members of R5 were in the studio working on music. In 2010 they released their *Ready Set Rock* **EP**, and in 2012 they signed a recording contract with Hollywood Records. Their first album for the label was *Louder*, which was released on September 24, 2013.

Ross and R5 were already a huge success, but it was only just the beginning!

FAVORITES

SPORTS: Ice hockey, skateboarding, surfing, **parkour**, and gymnastics

SKATE PARK: Pedlow in Los Angeles

MUSICAL ARTISTS: Justin Bieber, Bruno Mars, Michael Jackson, Led Zeppelin, The Script

HOLIDAY: Christmas

MOVIE BASED ON A BOOK/PLAY: Romeo and Juliet

BOARD GAME: Monopoly

COLOR: Yellow

DOG: Siberian husky

VIDEO GAME: Battlefield 3

WEATHER: Sunny beach days and rainy date days

SEASON: Winter

PIECE OF JEWELRY: His R5 necklace

GUM: Japanese gum—Lotte Black Black or Flavor Burst

ANIMATED MOVIE: Disney's Tarzan

EMOJI: "The scary purple dude with the smirk"

Teen Beach Movie costars Ross and Maia Mitchell help clean up the beach for the Heal the Bay event.

"I LOVE EVERY MUSICAL THAT'S EVER BEEN MADE!"

TRENDING: ROSS

WATCH HIS STAR RISE!

"**W**hen I booked [the role of Austin] on *Austin & Ally*, it changed my life," Ross told *J-14* magazine. Even though Ross and R5 were making big moves in the music world, *Austin & Ally* blasted open new doors for the young actor. "Every day someone says, 'Oh my gosh, you're Austin,'" Ross continued with *J-14*. "It's all very sweet."

Because *Austin & Ally* was part of the Disney world, Ross was also able to take on other big projects that helped build up his fan base. His social media profile grew every day. Ross became a trender on Instagram, Twitter, Facebook, Vine, and every other form of social media he touched.

Ross's popularity exploded when he starred in the hit Disney Channel movie *Teen Beach Movie* in July 2013. "I was super, super, super excited when I found out I was going to play the lead role

Tweet!
Ross's Twitter handle is @RossR5.

Teen Beach Movie costars Grace Phipps, Garrett Clayton, Maia Mitchell, and Ross pose for a shot.

in this movie," he told *Bop* magazine. "It's so cool that I'm in a movie, and I'm especially excited because it's a musical. *Teen Beach Movie* has all the aspects I would want in a movie. I think it's awesome!"

Another thing Ross loved about *Teen Beach Movie* was his character, Brady. "Brady is always chilling and just goes with the flow," he told *Bop* magazine. He also revealed that his favorite scene in the movie was

Ross's Timeline

Ross on the Rise

2009
R5 forms in Los Angeles

2010
R5 releases their debut EP, *Ready Set Rock*

FEBRUARY 28, 2011
Ross tapes the first episode of *Austin & Ally*

the "Cruisin' for a Bruisin'" dance scene, which had a definite *Grease* flavor. "When we were younger, my brothers and sister and I used to hang out in our basement and dress in leather jackets like in *Grease*," he said. "We'd dance and sing all of the songs from that movie. It's one of my favorites."

Speaking of favorites, when disneyme.com asked Ross what his most enjoyable moment on the *Teen Beach Movie* set was, he responded, "I can't pick just one moment. Every day was

Ross visits *Good Morning America* to promote *Teen Beach Movie*.

APRIL 6, 2011
The first episode of *Austin & Ally* airs

APRIL 2, 2012
Ross releases his solo single "A Billion Hits"

SEPTEMBER 12, 2012
Ross's soundtrack album for *Austin & Ally* is released

enjoyable! We were living near the sea in Puerto Rico. What's not to like about it?"

Teen Beach Movie was so successful that its creators began talking about a sequel right after the first movie aired in July 2013! In April 2014, Disney announced that *Teen Beach Movie 2*, starring the original cast, was scheduled to air in July 2015.

But what about R5? Things had really picked up for the band after they signed with Hollywood Records in 2012. They toured often and played countless shows for fans around the world. Between touring and acting, Ross's schedule was jam-packed. But in 2014, the Disney Channel announced that *Austin & Ally* would end after that season, in early 2015. Without the show taking up so much of his time, Ross was finally free to concentrate on music.

When asked to describe R5's sound, Ross explained to *Billboard*, "Our style is very pop/rock, but a little

FEBRUARY 19, 2013
R5's second EP, *Loud*, is released

MARCH 23, 2013
Ross wins big at the Nickelodeon Kids' Choice Awards for his performance on *Austin & Ally*

Ross, Rocky, and Riker make the crowd go wild at L.A.'s KISS FM's Wango Tango concert!

more guitar-driven with some really great melodies. My brothers are great writers, so it's pretty exciting to see it all come together."

You may have noticed that Ross always refers to the entire band when talking about his music. Even though

APRIL 27, 2013
Ross wins the Radio Disney Music Awards Best Music Video for "Heard It on the Radio"

JULY 19, 2013
Teen Beach Movie airs on the Disney Channel

SEPTEMBER 2, 2013
R5 makes their *Good Morning America* debut

R5 has the audience on their feet at the 2012 Magnificent Mile Lights Festival in Chicago.

he is the group's biggest star, he respects his bandmates. As a matter of fact, Ross told *J-14*, "Honestly, I don't like to be singled out from the band. I think it's cooler when the band is known instead of just one person—I'd rather it just be 'R5' and not 'Ross Lynch and R5.' We're all best friends. We're closer than anyone could be."

SEPTEMBER 24, 2013
R5's first full-length album, *Louder*, is released

MARCH 29, 2014
Ross wins another Nickelodeon Kids' Choice Award for *Austin & Ally*

AUGUST 10, 2014
Ross wins a Teen Choice Award for *Austin & Ally*

JANUARY 18, 2015
The first episode of *Austin & Ally's* fourth season premieres

And what about Ryland, the baby brother of the Lynch family? Well, because Ryland was too young to join the band when they first started back in Colorado, his siblings named him band manager. Ryland has grown into his "job." He told hopelessthunder.org, "As long as they do exactly what I tell them to do, there are no problems. They know who's the boss."

The fact is, there is no boss in R5. They have climbed to superstardom by working out any disagreements they

R5 are the ultimate jokesters.
They always keep you laughing.

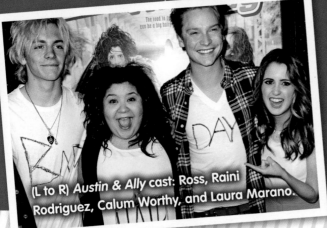

(L to R) Austin & Ally cast: Ross, Raini Rodriguez, Calum Worthy, and Laura Marano.

SPRING 2015
Sometime Last Night
is released

JUNE 26, 2015
Teen Beach Movie 2
premieres

You can't call R5 couch potatoes, but they love a mash-up!

might have had. Members express their own opinions, and compromises are made. "We're family first," Ross told *J-14*—and that includes Ellington Ratliff. "We all love each other and our parents raised us all to be best friends, and that's what we are. We'll be around for a long, long time."

Everything is decided as a group—especially business decisions. In 2014, R5 released the singles "Heart Made Up on You" and "Smile," and their second album, *Sometime Last Night*, was supposed to be released that fall. But because they wanted to give their very best, they pushed it back to 2015 and gave fans an early taste with "Let's Not Be Alone Tonight."

They are not going to release something just because someone says it's time. "We think everything's going at the right speed for us," Ross told *Billboard*. "You hear a lot of people say that the faster you rise, the faster you fall and I really do feel like R5 has had a really gradual rise and I hope we still rise and I hope we can also accumulate as many fans as possible. We've been a band for . . . years now, and we've gotten so much tighter and so much more experienced—everything that has to do with the band has just gotten so much better. . . . I feel like everything's going at the right speed. We know more now, and we're ready."

As for the new album, Ross added, "Our whole thing is to keep growing and to grow as people and a band. We like to have a lot of variety on our records. . . . We have all sorts of different things on the record, but we like that." And so do their fans!

Ryan Seacrest snaps a selfie with R5 and fans.

"MY MOM TELLS ME I WEAR MY HEART ON MY SLEEVE."

ROSS SPEAKS HIS MIND

STRAIGHT FROM HIS HEART . . . OUT OF HIS MOUTH

One really cool thing about Ross Lynch is that he isn't afraid to answer questions. He's glad to share all of his thoughts, whether they're serious or silly. Check out what he has to say about his fans' tweets, wanting to fly, skinny jeans, and lots more!

On Halloween costumes . . . "When we were little, our mom used to match us because she wanted us to feel like a team. [One year] we all dressed up as Zorro, all together . . . we all had our hats and swords and we were all sword fighting and all that stuff."

On musical training . . . "Actually, we [R5] are all self-taught musicians. But being a band for years, you learn quite a bit."

Skateboarding is one of Ross's favorite sports!

What he would do if he weren't a musician . . .

"I would have tried to be in the NHL [National Hockey League]. If I would have succeeded, that would have been great. If not, I'm really interested in aeronautical engineering. I don't really know much about it, but I've always been interested in it. And that also goes along with flying . . . I want to take lessons."

Magic!
Ross would love to be a magician.

On the best thing about being in R5 . . .

"Performing with these guys, definitely! I don't like having to perform by myself; being on stage with them is more fun."

On his favorite fan tweets . . . "I really like inspiring tweets, but really any tweet is a good tweet."

On being able to do magic . . . "It'd be really cool to do all types of magic. I'd snap my fingers and BOOM—be in Italy!"

On his nonmusic goals . . . "I have this dream to be a producer and director. I already have an idea for a film, but I can't tell you yet. It's a secret!"

On getting embarrassed . . . "Even if [something] would be embarrassing, for me it's not. I'm just like, 'Yup! I did it.'"

Did you know that R5 has toured in five of the seven continents?!!!

Advice for fans who want to get into the music biz . . . "Work hard, and don't give up! There are millions of people out there who want to be entertainers, so figure out what makes you unique, and capitalize on it. Most of all . . . enjoy the journey!"

On a literary character he would like to play in a movie . . . "Percy Jackson, but they've already made two [movies] with Logan Lerman. I'd take his job if he wants to give it up!"

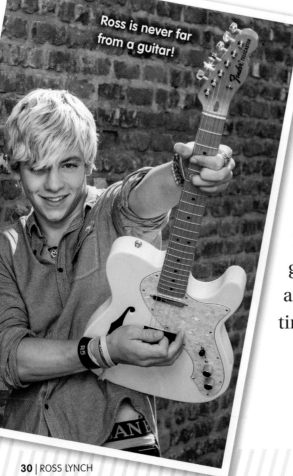

Ross is never far from a guitar!

On his favorite school subject . . . "I really like literature, 'cause I like words. I write songs. I'm an actor so I spend a lot of time with words. The tip is you can't skim over anything. If you want to get good grades, you have to read and read [the material] a few times, take your time with it."

On stage, Ross is living the dream he's had all his life!

On an on-stage embarrassing moment . . .

"A consistent embarrassing moment is forgetting lyrics when I'm on stage, especially since I write the songs! I forget my own lyrics. My excuse is John Lennon forgot lyrics all the time—it's something really creative people do."

On his middle school survival tips . . .

"Be yourself, get your friends and stick with them. Have their backs and they'll have yours."

Animal Lover
Ross encourages protecting endangered species.

On his skinny jeans collection . . . "I've got lots of different colors in my wardrobe. I've got hot pink skinny jeans, bright blue skinny jeans, green skinny jeans, patterned skinny jeans . . . You name them; I've got them!"

On his nicknames . . . "Recently, I've been called 'Batman' because I call my friend 'Robin.' But that's just me and him. Only I can call him 'Robin' and only he can call me 'Batman.' Some people call me Ross-some."

"JUST BEING REAL IS THE BEST WAY TO CATCH A PERSON'S EYE. I CAN TELL WHEN SOMEONE'S NOT BEING REAL."

Surfing is Ross's new passion!

On surfing . . . "Actually I learned to surf in order to play the part [of Brady in *Teen Beach Movie*]. I love it."

On the best thing about having a family band . . . "There is no filter, we can say whatever we want to each other and be honest. No one is going to get hurt feelings. We're always ourselves. We have each other's backs and feel confident that we have each other for support."

On his weird habits . . . "I sing all the time, is that a habit? Wait, no, I have a better one! I pull up my pants a lot. All the time! Even if they're not falling down, I randomly always pull them up. It's pretty weird."

On his perfect day off . . . "Surfing, lunch, movie, dinner, and hanging out with my family."

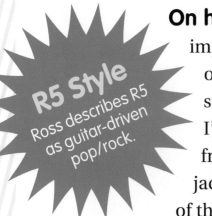

R5 Style
Ross describes R5 as guitar-driven pop/rock.

On how to impress a girl . . . "It's important [to be a gentleman]. I always open up doors. I try to do it all smooth, like if I see a door coming, I'll try to slowly, nonchalantly go in front of her and open it up. Take my jacket off when she's cold, that kind of thing."

On how to deal with bullies . . . "There're a lot of ways you could deal with bullies. Go tell someone, like a friend or an adult, or confront the person face-to-face. Just don't deal with it alone. . . . You have to keep in mind that people say things for attention. You'll be happier if you laugh everything off. Nobody else's opinion matters but your own. It all comes down to having confidence and always loving yourself!"

On not going to regular school . . . "I think I missed out on high school. . . . I want to be in a classroom where I can discuss and debate different things with other students. Getting a chance to be in a class full of intelligent people would be really cool."

On his relationship with his dad . . . "My dad is really good at giving 30-second speeches about what life is about."

On his dad's best advice . . . "It's that you get what you wish for. If you want to be something, you have to work hard at it and think about it."

On his artistic influences . . . "I'd say as far as musical influences. . . all the classics—Elvis [Presley], the Beatles, the [Rolling] Stones, Led Zeppelin, Bruce Springsteen— he's a huge inspiration. But current bands—I love Imagine Dragons, Walk the Moon, Young the Giant, Neon Trees, that sort of thing. And for acting, I don't really have any influences. I just feel it."

Believe it or not, a fan once gave Ross a goldfish!

ROSS LYNCH
MASH-UP
TRIVIA, FUN STUFF, MEGA FACTS, & MORE!

BEFORE A SHOW, THE MEMBERS OF R5 FORM A CIRCLE AND SHOUT, "READY! SET! GO!"

Ross
He's the passionate one in R5!

FOODIE FANTASIA

BREAKFAST
French toast

BREAKFAST RESTAURANT
The Griddle Café in Los Angeles

WORKDAY BREAKFAST
"Oatmeal with everything
in it and a bowl of fruit."

FAST-FOOD RESTAURANT
In-N-Out Burger

DRINK
Water

SANDWICH
Club sandwich

ICE CREAM FLAVOR
Chocolate chip cookie dough

PIZZA
Hawaiian

CANDY
Cadbury Creme Eggs, gummy bears,
Skittles, Swedish Fish

R5 ON R5

Ratliff on Rydel: "We like to call her the secret weapon of R5, because without her, we would just be another boy band. You know, who wants that? She brings the fun; she's really giggly."

Rydel on Riker: "Riker is our fearless leader. He's captain of the ship and he is a very hard worker, has the best work ethic ever, and he has a really cute nose."

Riker on Ross: "Ross is our awesome front man. He leads us in the shows in the front battlefield. Ross is very creative. He's a total artist. He's always striving for us to be different and try new things and definitely keeps us fresh."

Rocky on Ratliff: "He's the alien! Ratliff is the UFO in the group. . . . He's the only one not related. He probably has the biggest vocabulary in the group. He holds the fort down in the music because I'll follow him. Everyone follows the drums because he's kinda [the backbone]. He's also somewhat of a comedian as well. He's my sidekick."

Ross on Rocky: "Rocky can be quiet sometimes. He's also a thinker. He's very smart. He always did well in school. Good at math, which is probably why he's also very naturally musically talented. He's the one who started the whole music aspect of R5. He's the one who taught himself how to play the guitar first. . . . He's also really funny with a dry sense of humor."

IT'S ALL RELATIVE

Did you know that Ross and his siblings are first cousins of Derek and Julianne Hough from *Dancing with the Stars*? Though the Lynch family grew up in Colorado and the Houghs lived in Utah, they kept up with each other. Rydel remembers Stormie taking the kids to Las Vegas to see Derek and Julianne perform in dance competitions. Ross told *Access Hollywood*, "We're very close. We have good times together." And what about the rumor that Ross has been asked to appear on *DWTS*? He explained he thought about it but decided that he'd rather go on tour. Of course, he said that if he did go on the show, he "would probably kick some butt!"

THE MEMBERS OF R5 WEAR SNUGGIES ON THE TOUR BUS—REALLY!

FIRSTS

THING HE REACHES FOR IN THE REFRIGERATOR
Fruit

BOOK READ
Jonathan Livingston Seagull

CELEBRITY CRUSH
Olivia Hussey from the 1968 movie *Romeo and Juliet*

KISS
When he was 13

DAY OF SCHOOL
"I had one teacher in elementary school I didn't particularly like, but my brother loved his teacher and said, 'Dude, come into my class.' I did, but the teacher didn't let me stay."

WORD GAMES

FAVORITE WORD: Awesome
FAVORITE WAY TO READ: Paperback books
THREE WORDS TO DESCRIBE HIMSELF:
"Creative . . . Opinionated . . . Thinker."

HARDEST WORD TO PRONOUNCE AS A KID
ROSS: His brother Riker's name—he called him "Yiker." He also had trouble with the letter L—he pronounced "Ally" as "Awie."
RIKER: Whiskers—he said "Wishers."
RATLIFF: On purpose—he said "on porpoise."
RYDEL: Beautiful—she said "Bootiful."
ROCKY: Riker—he called his brother "Iker."

Ross jams at the House of Blues in Cleveland, Ohio.

ROSS PREDICTIONS

WHAT'S IN STORE FOR THIS GOLDEN BOY?

One thing is for sure: Music will always be a major part of Ross's life. Ross doesn't see R5 breaking up anytime soon. Instead, they've got big plans for the future. Shortly before the release of their second album, Ross said they had always fantasized about a worldwide stadium tour. Of course, there also is the dream of a Grammy or two.

Ross thinks R5 is ready for the next big step. They have worked hard to evolve with their growing fandom. "Our goal is to grow as a band and to not limit ourselves," Ross told *J-14*. "[Our] songs are a lot more mature. Everyone in the band has gotten older and our musical influences have changed a lot. I've especially changed since the last album going from 15 to 18 years old. I feel like those few years are almost the biggest turning point in your life!"

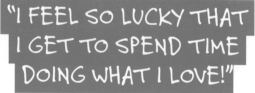

"I FEEL SO LUCKY THAT I GET TO SPEND TIME DOING WHAT I LOVE!"

It's obvious that Ross has put a lot of thought into his future. When disneyme.com asked him where he would like to see himself in 10 years, he quickly replied, "Hopefully, I'll be doing feature films and it would be awesome if R5 was putting out their sixth album. Maybe I'll be on a huge world tour with the band, too? I hope that I'll be doing everything I'm doing now, but on a much bigger scale. Bigger movies, bigger tours, and bigger gigs. We'll just have to wait and see!"

You may have noticed that Ross mentioned feature films, and you can rest

Ross would love to collaborate with Bruno Mars!

Ross loves to stop and meet his fans—wherever he is!

assured that he has a laser beam-like focus on the big screen. After working on the made-for-TV *Teen Beach Movie* and *Teen Beach Movie 2*, Ross has his heart set on a theatrical film for his next project. His **agent** has received tons of possible scripts. They just have to search out the right one for Ross. And, as this *Real Bio* is being written, there is buzz that they may have found it! According to a Hollywood trade magazine, Ross will be starring in a comedy from the writer of *17 Again*—a movie that opened a lot of doors for Zac Efron. This movie could do the same for Ross!

"I WISH I LIVED IN THE '60S. I LIKE THE MUSIC . . . THE CLOTHING WAS JUST SO FUN."

Even while he is part of R5 and acting, Ross is thinking about working behind the camera. "I kind of have this dream to direct and produce my own movie," Ross told *Bop*. "I'm always on set or on a stage, so I'm always observing what people do and how they solve their problems." Ross told *Just Dance* magazine, "I would love to start my own production company at some point, as well as write and direct."

Sounds like Ross has everything mapped out. Even though he knows there might be detours, he's ready to rock the road to superstardom!

"SLEEP WHEN YOU'RE DEAD" IS ONE OF THE ENERGETIC ROSS'S MOTTOES!

As for the future? Ross says, "I just want to keep doing acting and music!"

Resources

BOOK

Schwartz, Heather E. *Ross Lynch: Actor, Singer, Dancer, Superstar*. Minneapolis: Lerner Publications, 2015.

ARTICLES

Buchanan, Kirsten and Deepika Rajani. "INTERVIEW: Teen Beach Movie Star Ross Lynch Talks Going On A Date With Demi Lovato, Who His Leading Lady Would Be And Harry Styles" New York: Entertainmentwise.com, 2013.

Lewis, Casey. "It's Official: Ross Lynch Is the Next Zac Efron," New York, *Teen Vogue*, 2013.

Facts for Now

Visit this Scholastic Web site for more information on **Ross Lynch**: www.factsfornow.scholastic.com
Enter the keywords **Ross Lynch**

Glossary

agent *(AY-juhnt)* someone who works with actors, singers, and other entertainers to help them find work

audition *(aw-DISH-uhn)* give a short performance to compete for a part in a play, film, or television show

cameo *(KAM-ee-oh)* a small character part in a play or a movie, usually played by a famous actor or actress

EP *(EE PEE)* short for "extended play"; an EP is shorter than a full album but longer than a single

parkour *(par-KOOR)* a sport based on passing through a variety of obstacles to reach a goal in the fastest way possible

Index

Acknowledgments

Page 8: Kids' names: *Bop* January/February 2014
Page 9: Ross dancing: *Bop* September 2014
Page 9: Stormie on Ross: *Bop* June/July 2014
Page 10: Ross in restaurant: *J-14* October/November 2014; Ross and family shows: *Twist*
Page 11: Glee club: *Twist*
Page 15: Emoji: *Bop* April 2013
Page 17: Audience: JustJaredJr.com June 26, 2013
Page 17: Booked on *Austin & Ally*: *J-14* October/November 2013; Very sweet: *J-14* October/November 2013; *Teen Beach Movie* lead: *Bop* August 2013
Page 18: Brady: *Bop* August 2013
Pages 19–20: Puerto Rico set: disneyme.com
Page 20–21: R5's sound: *Billboard* August 2012
Page 22: Just be R5: *J-14* October/November 2013

Page 23: Ryland: hopelessthunder.org July 18, 2011
Page 24: Best friends: *J-14* February 2014; New album: *Billboard* October 31, 2014
Page 26: Heart on my sleeve: *Tiger Beat* April 2013
Page 27: Halloween costumes: Scholastic interview June 2014; Musical training: Scholastic interview June 2014
Page 28: If he weren't a musician: Scholastic interview 2014; Best thing about R5: musichel.com January 8, 2013
Page 29: Fan tweets: *Popstar* November 2012; Magic: *Bop* February 2013; Goals: *Bop* February 2013; Embarrassed: *J-14* March 2013
Page 30: Advice: JustJaredJr.com June 26, 2013; Percy Jackson: Scholastic interview October 3, 2013; Favorite subject: Scholastic interview October 3, 2013

Page 31: Embarrassing moment: Scholastic interview October 3, 2013; Middle school: Scholastic interview October 3, 2013
Page 32: Crazy: *Bop* June/July 2013; Being real: *J-14* August 2013; Skinny jeans: disneyme.org; Nicknames: Fanlala.com July 16, 2013
Page 33: Surfing: *Teen Now* October 2013; Family band: *Teen Now* October 2013; Weird habits: *Bop* September 2012
Page 34: Perfect day: *Glitter* Fall 2013; Impress a girl: *J-14* August 2013; Bullies: *Tiger Beat* December 2014; High school: *Bop* April 2014
Page 35: Relationship with dad: *Tiger Beat* April 2015; Best advice: *Tiger Beat* April 2015; Artistic influences: Fanlala.com July 16, 2013
Page 37: Workday breakfast: *J-14* March 2013

Pages 38-39: R5 on R5: Scholastic interview June 2014
Page 40: It's all relative: *Access Hollywood*
Page 41: First day of school: Scholastic interview October 3, 2012; Ross's self-description: Scholastic interview October 3, 2012; Hardest word to pronounce: Fanlala.com July 16, 2013; Biggest fear: *Bop* September 2012
Page 43: Goal: *J-14* October/November 2012; 10 years from now: disneyme.com; Lucky: *Twist* December 2013
Page 44: '60s blurb: *Girls' Life* August 2013
Page 45: Producer/director: *Bop* April 2014; Production company: *Just Dance* June 2013; Sleep: Scholastic handwritten fact sheet 2014; Acting and music: *Teen Now* October 2013

About the Author

Marie Morreale is the author of many official and unofficial celebrity biographies. She attended New York University as an English/creative writing major and began her writing and editorial career in New York City. As the editor of teen/music magazines *Teen Machine* and *Jam!*, she covered TV, film, and music personalities and interviewed superstars such as Michael Jackson, Britney Spears, and Justin Timberlake/*NSYNC. Morreale was also an editor/writer at Little Golden Books.

Today, she is the executive editor, Media, of Scholastic Classroom Magazines writing about pop-culture, sports, news, and special events. Morreale lives in New York City and is entertained daily by her two Maine coon cats, Cher and Sullivan.